ORIGAMI with DOLLAR BILLS:

Another Way to Impress People with Your Money

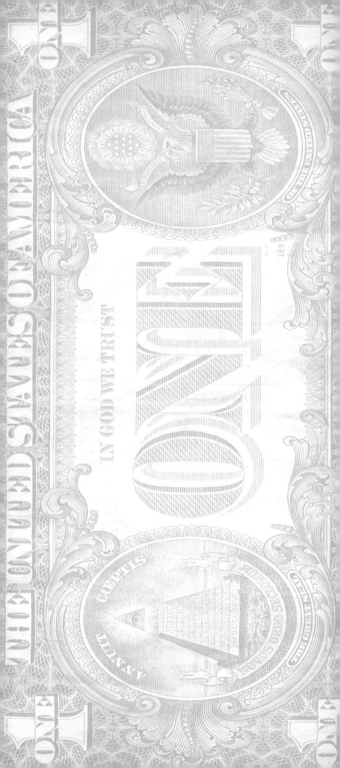

ORIGAMI with DOLLAR BILLS:

Another Way to Impress People with Your Money

by Duy Nguyen

Sterling Publishing Co., Inc.
New York

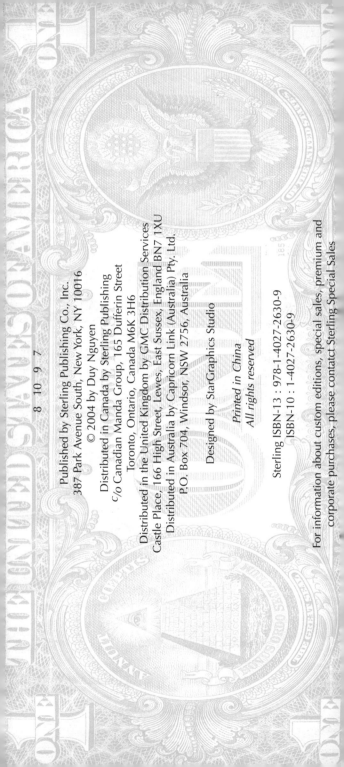

Published by Sterling Publishing Co., Inc.
387 Park Avenue South, New York, NY 10016
© 2004 by Duy Nguyen
Distributed in Canada by Sterling Publishing
c/o Canadian Manda Group, 165 Dufferin Street
Toronto, Ontario, Canada M6K 3H6
Distributed in the United Kingdom by GMC Distribution Services
Castle Place, 166 High Street, Lewes, East Sussex, England BN7 1XU
Distributed in Australia by Capricorn Link (Australia) Pty. Ltd.
P.O. Box 704, Windsor, NSW 2756, Australia

Designed by StarGraphics Studio

Printed in China
All rights reserved

Sterling ISBN-13 : 978-1-4027-2630-9
ISBN-10 : 1-4027-2630-9

For information about custom editions, special sales, premium and
corporate purchases, please contact Sterling Special Sales

TABLE OF CONTENTS

INTRODUCTION

Origami with Dollar Bills: Another Way to Impress People with Your Money offers a unique twist to traditional origami projects. Using a dollar bill instead of conventional origami paper, you don't have to look further than your wallet and beyond your hands in order to create 15 fabulous origami objects. The projects, ranging from a horseshoe crab, to a Jedi, to an oriental dragon are fun and clever and are guaranteed to amaze everyone. Although some of the projects are more challenging than others, with a bit of patience and practice, without a doubt you will soon master them.

To make the folds that are mentioned in the step-by-step instructions of each project, refer to the Basic Folds section, pages 9-12. The origami projects are arranged according to how many dollar bills you will need. Beginning on page 13, the first six projects use only one dollar bill and don't involve any attachments. But don't be fooled, they still require some very intricate folding. The following six projects, starting on page 35, are made by attaching two parts—each made from a dollar—together, while the last three origami objects, from page 63 on, consist of three attachments made from single dollar bills. Don't worry, it's not necessary to cut, glue, tape, or deface the currency in any way so you won't be committing vandalism!

INTRODUCTION

Throughout *Origami with Dollar Bills*, you will learn amazing facts about United States currency and its rich history, so to speak: from how many times a dollar bill can be folded before tearing, to how many dollar bills stacked together equal a mile, to why only green ink is used. For more great information and fascinating trivia about United States currency, check out the Bureau of Engraving and Printing's website, www.moneyfactory.com.

So, have a little fun and at the same time exercise your mind and your fingers using *Origami with Dollar Bills*. And don't forget to show the world what money can really do!

BASIC FOLDS & SYMBOLS

VALLEY FOLD

1. Fold along the dotted line

2. Completed Valley Fold

MOUNTAIN FOLD

1. Fold to the back

2. Completed Mountain Fold

Fold Line

Mountain Fold Line

Hidden Fold Line

Fold in This Direction

Turn Over or Rotate

Fold Then Unfold

Pleat Fold

Crease Line

BASIC FOLDS & SYMBOLS

INSIDE REVERSE FOLD

OUTSIDE REVERSE FOLD

1.

2. Completed Inside Reverse Fold

1.

2. Completed Outside Reverse Fold

PLEAT FOLD

1. Valley folds   2. Valley fold   3. Pleat Fold

PLEAT FOLD REVERSE

1. Valley folds   2. Valley fold   3. Pleat Fold Reverse

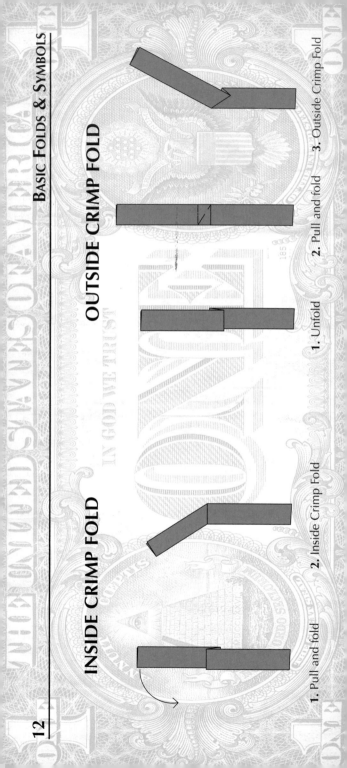

INSIDE CRIMP FOLD

1. Pull and fold

2. Inside Crimp Fold

OUTSIDE CRIMP FOLD

1. Unfold

2. Pull and fold

3. Outside Crimp Fold

ONE DOLLAR OBJECTS

SEA LION

1. Valley fold in half and unfold

2. Repeat

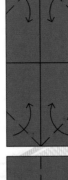

3. Valley folds

4. Turn over to the other side

5. Valley folds

6. Repeat

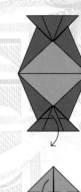

7. Valley fold

8. Repeat

9. Valley folds and squash folds

10. Valley fold in half

11. Valley fold and unfold

12. Repeat

13. Crimp fold along the creased line

14. Inside reverse fold

15. Valley fold both sides

SEA LION

18. Completed Sea Lion

16. Valley fold both sides

17. Valley fold to turn head

KLINGON BIRD OF PREY

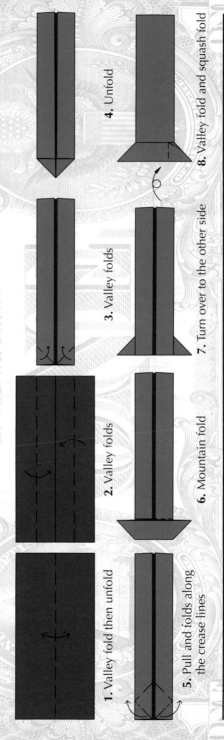

1. Valley fold then unfold

2. Valley folds

3. Valley folds

4. Unfold

5. Pull and folds along the crease lines

6. Mountain fold

7. Turn over to the other side

8. Valley fold and squash fold

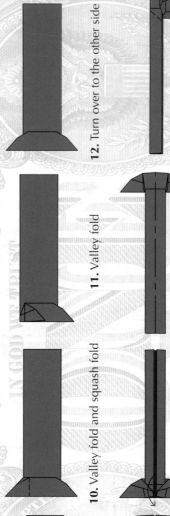

9. Valley fold

10. Valley fold and squash fold

11. Valley fold

12. Turn over to the other side

13. Valley fold

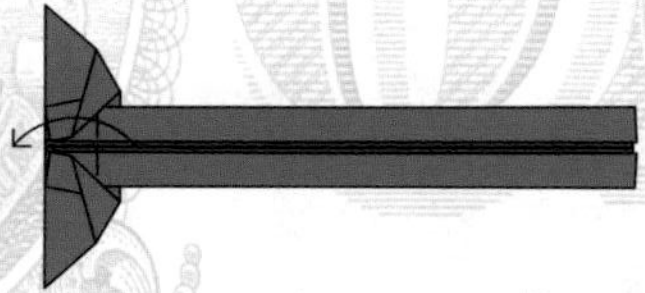

14. Valley fold

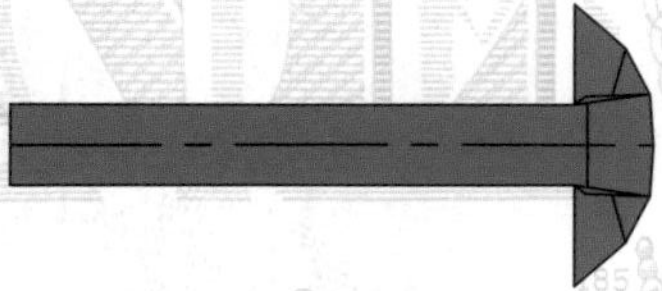

15. Mountain fold in half

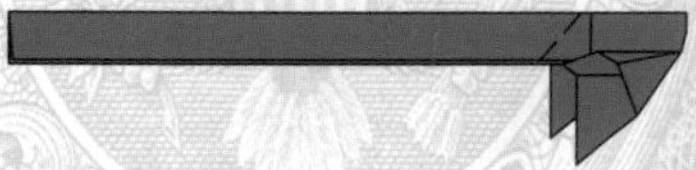

16. Valley folds

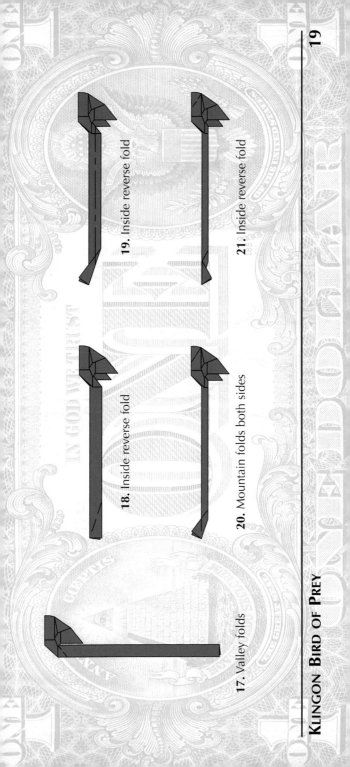

17. Valley folds

18. Inside reverse fold

19. Inside reverse fold

20. Mountain folds both sides

21. Inside reverse fold

KLINGON BIRD OF PREY

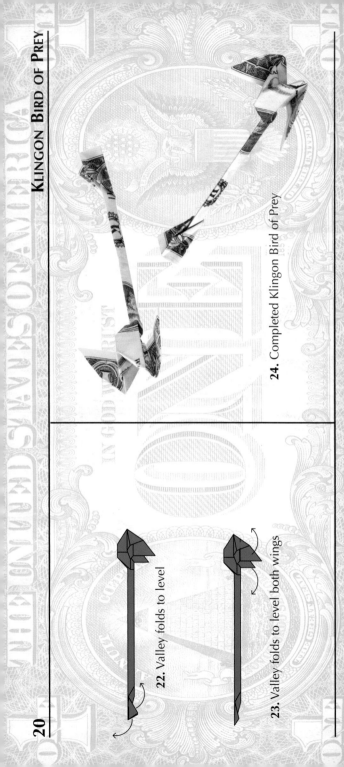

24. Completed Klingon Bird of Prey

22. Valley folds to level

23. Valley folds to level both wings

ELECTRIC EEL

1. Start with one dollar bill; fold in half and unfold

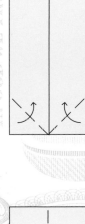

2. Valley folds

4. Repeat

5. Valley fold

3. Valley fold

6. Valley fold and hide behind layer

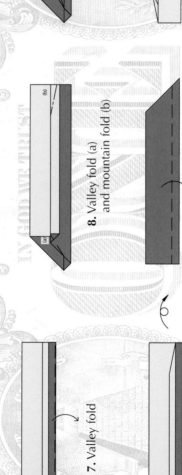

7. Valley fold

10. Turn over to the other side

8. Valley fold (a) and mountain fold (b)

11. Valley fold

9. Valley fold

12. Mountain fold

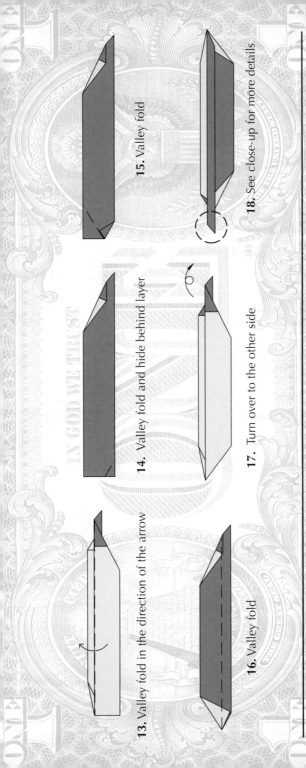

13. Valley fold in the direction of the arrow

14. Valley fold and hide behind layer

15. Valley fold

16. Valley fold

17. Turn over to the other side

18. See close-up for more details

26. Valley fold

22. Valley folds

25. Valley fold

21. Valley folds

20. Pull down as shown

24. Turn over

19. Crimp folds

23. Valley fold

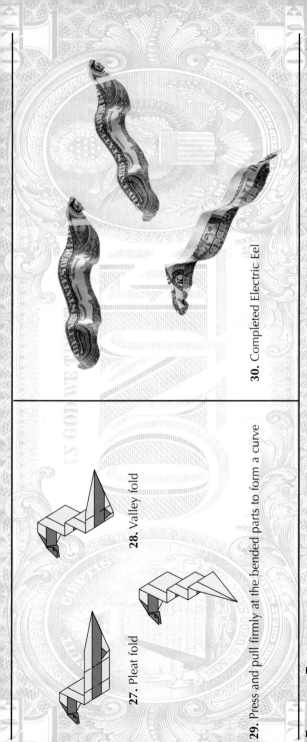

27. Pleat fold

28. Valley fold

29. Press and pull firmly at the bended parts to form a curve

30. Completed Electric Eel

ELECTRIC EEL

FUN FACTS ABOUT DOLLAR BILLS

$ *You can double fold (first forward and then backwards) a bill 4000 times before it will tear.*

$ *Green with Envy: Green ink was originally used in the mid-1800s to deter counterfeiters from photographing currency—then photographs were only black and white. Green ink continued to be used for several reasons. First, a special formula had been developed that was highly resistant to chemical and physical changes. Second, it was plentiful. And third, psychologically, green was identified with a strong and stable Government.*

$ *A bill is 25% linen and 75% cotton.*

$ Bills are made using a process called intaglio printing, which creates the effect of a slightly raised front and a slightly indented back. Each of the Bureau of Engraving's 24 presses, located in Fort Worth, Texas and Washington, D.C., is capable of printing over 8,000 sheets per hour.

$ Together, the Fort Worth, Texas and Washington D.C. presses use 18 tons of ink, per day.

$ Have you ever wanted your picture on a dollar bill? Well, not in your lifetime! No, seriously, after the Chief of the Bureau of Engraving and Printing, L.M. Clark, selected his own visage to appear on a 50-cent note, there was so much uproar that an act of Congress prohibiting the use of portraits of any living persons, was passed on April 7, 1866.

FUN FACTS ABOUT DOLLAR BILLS

HORSESHOE CRAB

1. Valley fold in half

2. Valley fold and unfold

3. Inside reverse folds

4. Valley folds

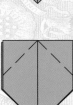

5. Valley fold

6. Repeat

7. Mountain folds

8. Turn over

9. Mountain fold

10. Rotate and turn over

11. Swing over flap, allowing squashes

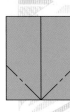

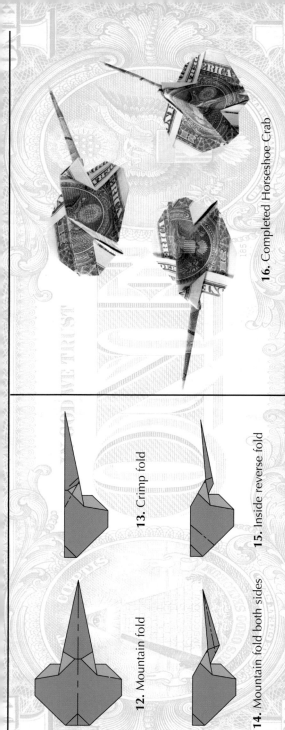

12. Mountain fold

13. Crimp fold

14. Mountain fold both sides

15. Inside reverse fold

16. Completed Horseshoe Crab

HORSESHOE CRAB

PHOENIX

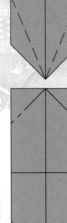

1. Valley fold and unfold

2. Repeat

3. Mountain folds

4. Valley folds

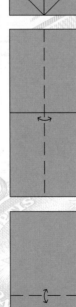

5. Valley fold in half

6. Valley fold and unfold

7. Valley fold and unfold

8. Crimp fold

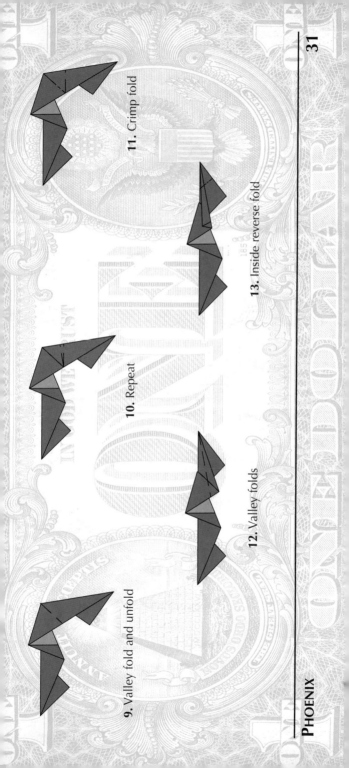

9. Valley fold and unfold

10. Repeat

11. Crimp fold

12. Valley folds

13. Inside reverse fold

PHOENIX

31

18. Completed Phoenix

15. Crimp fold

17. Rotate

14. Squash folds

16. Inside reverse fold

VAMPIRE BAT

1. Valley fold

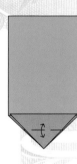

3. Valley fold and unfold

4. Sink

2. Inside reverse folds

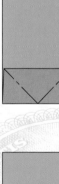

5. Mountain folds

6. Valley folds and hide

7. Mountain fold

8. Valley folds

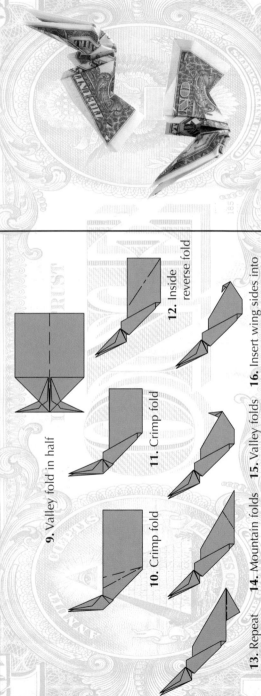

9. Valley fold in half

10. Crimp fold

11. Crimp fold

12. Inside reverse fold

13. Repeat

14. Mountain folds

15. Valley folds

16. Insert wing sides into each other; rotate model

17. Completed Vampire Bat

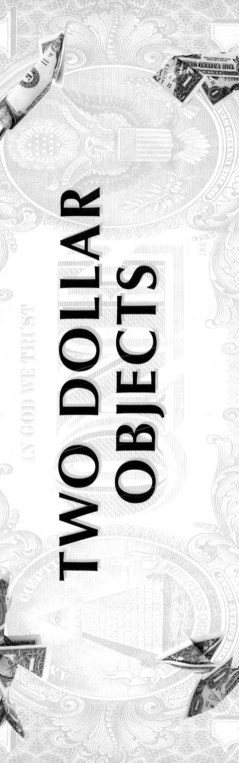

TWO DOLLAR OBJECTS

PART 1

2. Squash fold

3. Mountain fold

4. Pull and fold

5. Inside reverse fold

6. Rotate

7. Valley-fold both sides

8. Completed Part 1

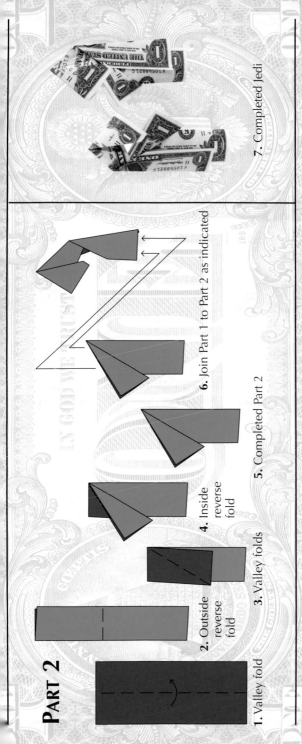

PART 2

1. Valley fold

2. Outside reverse fold

3. Valley folds

4. Inside reverse fold

5. Completed Part 2

6. Join Part 1 to Part 2 as indicated

7. Completed Jedi

FUN FACTS ABOUT DOLLAR BILLS

$ Of the notes printed each year, 95% are used to replace notes already in circulation. 45% of the notes printed are $1 bills.

$ The $2 bill first was authorized by the Continental Congress on June 25, 1776, over a week before the Declaration of Independence was signed, but Thomas Jefferson's portrait did not appear on the bill until 1928. A special $2 bill was commissioned in 1976 to celebrate the United States Bicentennial. On the back of the bill, an engraving of John Trumbull's painting, "The Signing of the Declaration of Independence" replaced the image of Monticello that had appeared on the bill since 1963.

$ A pound of currency would include 454 bills, regardless of denomination. Each note weighs one gram.

$ If each bill ever printed was laid end to end, they would stretch around the equator about 24 times.

**$** From studying old manuscripts, historians suspect that the "$" came about by writing "S" over "P" for the Spanish peso or pieces of eight, their currency. This symbol was widely accepted before the adoption of the United States dollar in 1785.

FUN FACTS ABOUT DOLLAR BILLS

TIGER SHARK

PART 1

1. Valley fold and unfold

2. Valley fold and unfold

3. Valley fold

4. Valley fold

5. Valley fold

6. Valley fold

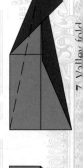

7. Valley fold

8. Valley fold

9. Valley fold

10. Crimp folds and valley fold in half

11. Outside reverse fold

12. Pleat folds both sides

13. Valley fold both the front and back

14. Repeat

15. Completed Part 1

TIGER SHARK

Part 2

4. Valley fold

8. Valley fold both sides

3. Valley fold

7. Outside reverse fold

2. Valley fold

6. Valley fold in half

1. Valley fold and unfold

5. Valley fold

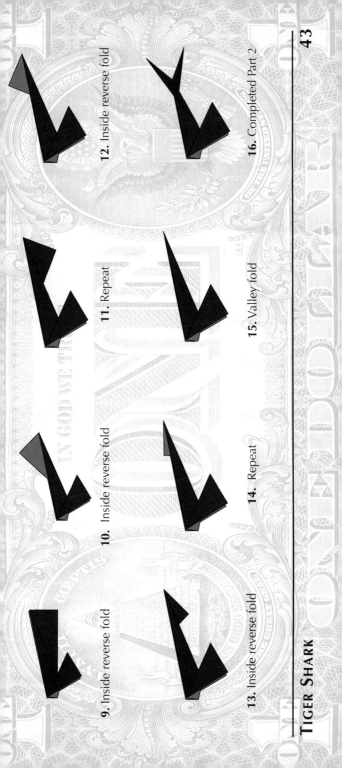

9. Inside reverse fold

10. Inside reverse fold

11. Repeat

12. Inside reverse fold

13. Inside reverse fold

14. Repeat

15. Valley fold

16. Completed Part 2

TIGER SHARK

ATTACHMENT

1. Join both parts together as indicated by the arrows

2. Press firmly at the tail bend to ensure the attachment of both parts

3. Completed Tiger Shark.

SQUID

PART 1

1. Valley fold in half

2. Valley fold and unfold

3. Inside reverse folds

4. Pull and fold

5. Squash folds

6. Inside reverse folds

7. Repeat

8. Pull and fold

9. Completed Part 1 of Squid

PART 2

4. Valley folds

9. Completed Part 2

3. Mountain folds

8. Turn over

7. Layer insert

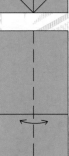

2. Repeat

6. Valley fold

1. Valley fold and unfold

5. Valley fold

Attachment

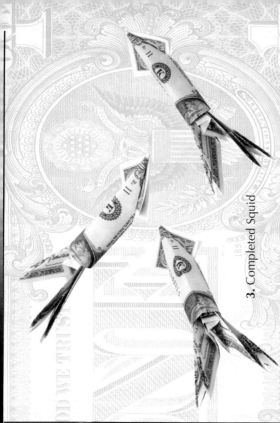

1. Insert Part 1 into opening of Part 2 as indicated

2. Mountain fold and unfold

3. Completed Squid

Squid

Fruit Bat

PART 1

1. Valley folds and unfolds

2. Valley folds and unfolds

3. Valley folds

4. Inside reverse folds

5. Mountain fold

6. Inside reverse fold

7. Valley fold

8. Repeat

9. Squash fold

10. Valley fold

11. Repeat

13. Valley fold

14. Valley fold

15. Valley folds

12. Squash fold

16. Mountain folds

17. Inside reverse

18. Outside reverse

19. Completed Part 1

FRUIT BAT

FRUIT BAT

PART 2

1. Valley fold in half

2. Valley fold and unfold

3. Inside reverse folds

4. Valley folds

5. Turn over to the other side

6. Pleat folds

7. Completed Part 2

ATTACHMENT

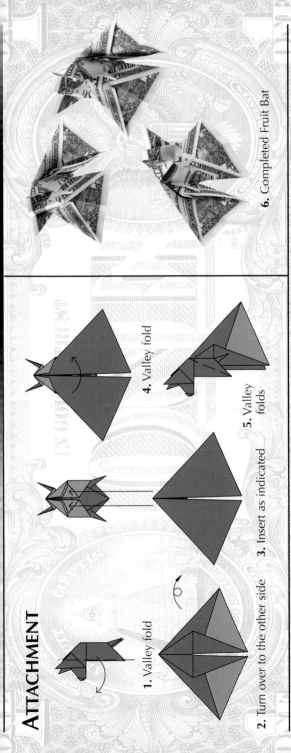

1. Valley fold

2. Turn over to the other side   3. Insert as indicated

4. Valley fold

5. Valley folds

6. Completed Fruit Bat

FRUIT BAT

FUN FACTS ABOUT DOLLAR BILLS

$ The Bureau of Engraving and Printing produces 37 million notes a day, with a face value of approximately $696 million.

$ The lifespan of a bill depends on its denomination: A $1 bill, lasting for approximately 22 months, tends to die young, while $50 and $100 bills have the longest existence, with a survival rate of approximately nine years. On average, a $20 bill will make it through one presidential term, four years, whereas $5 bills last half of that. The life of the $10 bill is approximately three years.

$ Each bill has a thickness of .0043 inches; a stack of bills one mile high would contain over 14 million currency notes.

$ So why do only people and places appear on currency?
As a government agency, the Bureau of Engraving and Printing cannot endorse and thus reproduce the likeness of any commercial product or firm. But what about the four automobiles on the back of the $10 bill that are supposed to be Model "T's"? While nothing says American pride more than Ford, the cars are of no specific make or model; rather, they are composites of cars produced in the 1920s, when the vignette was completed.

$ It costs approximately 4.2 cents to produce each bill.

FUN FACTS ABOUT DOLLAR BILLS

EUROPEAN DRAGON

PART 1

1. Valley fold

2. Valley fold and unfold

3. Valley folds

4. Valley folds

5. Valley fold

6. Crimp fold

7. See blow-up for more details

8. Crimp fold

9. Valley fold

10. Valley folds

11. Outside reverse

12. Zoom out

13. Inside reverse fold

14. Mountain fold

15. Repeat

16. Completed Part 1

EUROPEAN DRAGON

PART 2

EUROPEAN DRAGON

1. Valley fold in half

2. Valley fold and unfold

3. Inside reverse folds

4. Valley folds

5. Turn over to the other side

6. Valley folds

7. Mountain fold in half

8. Completed Part 2

ATTACHMENT

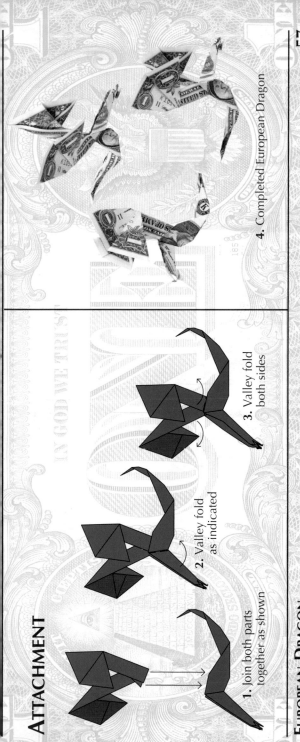

1. Join both parts together as shown

2. Valley fold as indicated

3. Valley fold both sides

4. Completed European Dragon

EUROPEAN DRAGON

EAGLE

PART 1

1. Valley fold

2. Inside reverse folds

3. Valley fold and unfold

4. Sink

5. Valley fold

6. Valley fold and unfold

7. Valley fold

8. Repeat

9. Valley fold

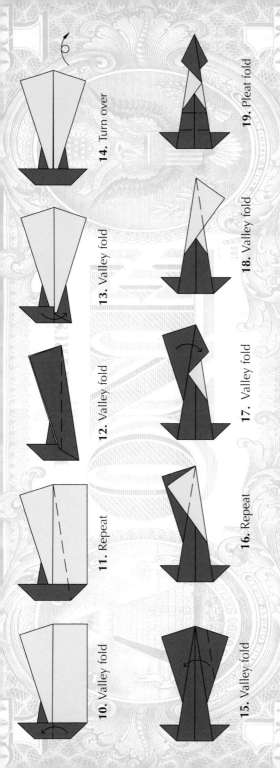

10. Valley fold

11. Repeat

12. Valley fold

13. Valley fold

14. Turn over

15. Valley fold

16. Repeat

17. Valley fold

18. Valley fold

19. Pleat fold

EAGLE

20. Valley fold in half

21. Valley folds

22. Valley folds

23. Inside reverse folds

24. Inside reverse folds

25. Crimp fold

26. Valley folds

27. Outside reverse fold

28. Valley folds

29. Completed Part 1

PART 2

1. Valley fold and unfold

2. Valley fold

3. Valley fold

4. Repeat

5. Valley fold

6. Turn over

7. Valley fold

8. Valley fold

9. Outside reverse fold

10. Crimp folds

11. Inside reverse fold

12. Completed Part 2

EAGLE

ATTACHMENT

1. Insert Part 2 into Part 1 as indicated

2. Mountain fold both sides

3. Completed Eagle

THREE DOLLAR OBJECTS

ROGER'S RABBIT

PART 1

1. Valley folds

2. Valley fold and unfold

3. Valley folds

4. Valley folds

PART 2

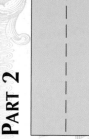

1. Valley folds

2. Inside reverse folds

3. Mountain fold top and valley folds the sides; repeat behind

4. Swing over a flap at each side

5. Valley fold; repeat behind

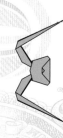

10. Turn over

11. Valley folds

12. Pleat fold

13. Completed Part 1

ROGER'S RABBIT

6. Valley fold; repeat behind

7. Valley fold; repeat behind

8. Valley fold; repeat behind

9. Valley fold sides to center; repeat behind

10. Swing over a flap at each side

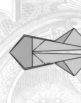

11. Inside reverse folds

12. Valley folds

13. Valley folds

14. Valley folds

15. Mountain folds

16. Completed Part 2

PART 3

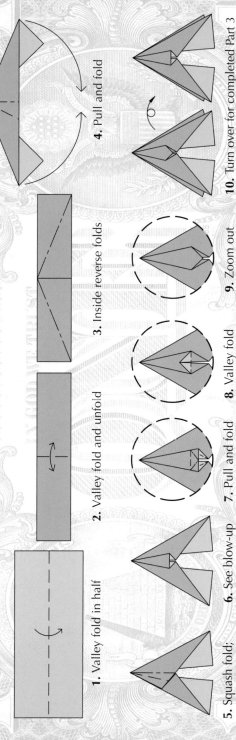

1. Valley fold in half

2. Valley fold and unfold

3. Inside reverse folds

4. Pull and fold

5. Squash fold; repeat behind

6. See blow-up

7. Pull and fold

8. Valley fold

9. Zoom out

10. Turn over for completed Part 3

ROGER'S RABBIT

ATTACHMENT

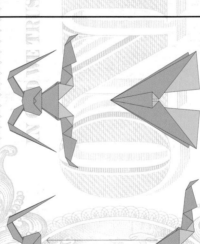

1. Valley fold

2. Completed First Attachment; now join with Part 3.

3. Completed Roger's Rabbit.

PART 1

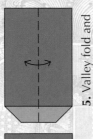

1. Valley fold

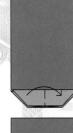

2. Inside reverse folds

3. Sink

4. Valley fold

5. Valley fold and unfold

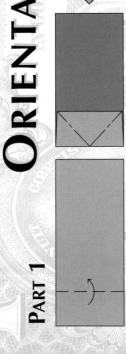

6. Valley fold

7. Repeat

8. Valley fold

9. Valley folds

10. Repeat

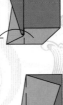

11. Valley fold

12. Valley fold

13. Fold in half

14. Valley fold both sides

15. Inside reverse fold

PART 2

1. Start with step 4 Part 1; then mountain fold

2. Valley fold both sides

3. Inside reverse folds

4. Inside reverse folds

5. Valley fold both sides

6. Valley fold both sides

7. Inside reverse folds

8. Completed Part 2

ORIENTAL DRAGON

PART 3

1. Valley fold and unfold

2. Valley fold

3. Valley fold

4. Repeat

5. Valley fold

6. Repeat steps 3 to 4

7. Valley folds

8. Fold in half

9. Completed Part 3

ATTACHMENT

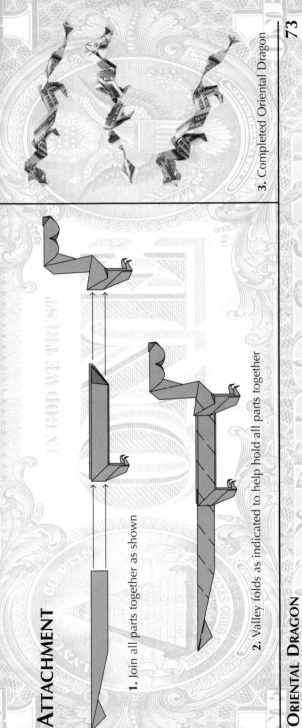

1. Join all parts together as shown

2. Valley folds as indicated to help hold all parts together

3. Completed Oriental Dragon

FUN FACTS ABOUT DOLLAR BILLS

$ The largest note ever printed by the Bureau of Engraving and Printing was the $100,000 Gold Certificate, Series 1934. Printed for 3 weeks, from December 18, 1934 through January 9, 1935, they were not circulated among the general public but rather were used for transactions between Federal Reserve Banks.

$ Since 1969, the largest bill in circulation has been the $100 bill.

$ While Susan B. Anthony and more recently Sacagawea have appeared on the half-dollar and one-dollar coins, Martha Washington is the only woman whose portrait has appeared on a bill: First on the front of the $1 Silver Certificate in 1886 and 1891 and then on the back of the $1 Silver Certificate of 1896.

$ If you had 10 billion $1 bills, and spent one every second of every day, it would require 317 years for you to go broke. It would take a lot longer to make origami objects with those 10 billion bills.

FUN FACTS ABOUT DOLLAR BILLS

SCORPION

PART 1

1. Valley fold in half

2. Inside reverse folds; turn over

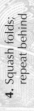

3. Pull and fold

4. Squash folds; repeat behind

PART 2

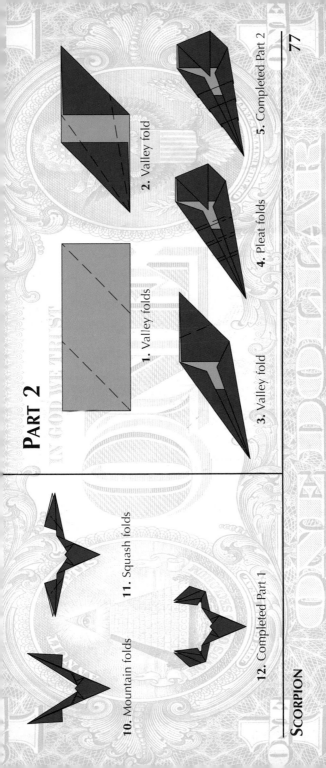

1. Valley folds

2. Valley fold

3. Valley fold

4. Pleat folds

5. Completed Part 2

10. Mountain folds

11. Squash folds

12. Completed Part 1

PART 3

1. Valley fold in half

2. Inside reverse

3. Push and fold

4. Pleat fold; repeat behind

5. Inside reverse fold; repeat behind

6. Repeat step 3; repeat behind

7. Inside reverse

8. Rotate

9. Valley folds two layers at each side;

10. Valley fold; repeat behind

11. Hide behind layers; repeat behind

12. Separate legs

13. Completed Part 3

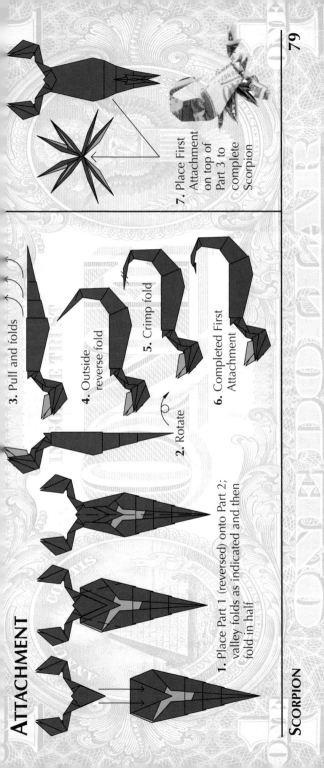

ATTACHMENT

1. Place Part 1 (reversed) onto Part 2; valley folds as indicated and then fold in half

2. Rotate

3. Pull and folds

4. Outside reverse fold

5. Crimp fold

6. Completed First Attachment

7. Place First Attachment on top of Part 3 to complete Scorpion

SCORPION

INDEX

185